The Story & Legend of Hiram Abiff

By William Harvey, Manly P. Hall and Albert G. Mackey

Copyright © 2019 Lamp of Trismegistus. All rights reserved. No part of this publication may be reproduced or transmitted in any form or by any means, electronic or mechanical, including photocopying, recording, or by any information storage and retrieval system, without permission in writing from Hecate Arcanum. Reviewers may quote brief passages.

ISBN: 978-1-63118-411-6

Foundations of Freemasonry Series

Other Books in this Series and Related Titles

Symbolism and Discourses on the Entered Apprentice, Fellowcraft and Master Mason Blue Lodge Degrees
by H. L. Haywood, Asahel W. Gage, William Harvey, Albert G. Mackey and Arthur Edward Waite (978-1-63118-413-0)

Symbolism of the Corner Stone, the North East Corner and the Religious & Masonic Symbolism of Stones by Albert G. Mackey, William Harvey and William Wynn Westcott
(978-1-63118-412-3)

Ancient Mysteries and Secret Societies by Manly P. Hall
(978-1-63118-410-9)

The Influence of Pythagoras on Freemasonry, the Golden Verses of Pythagoras and the Life and Philosophy of Pythagoras by Albert G. Mackey and Manly P. Hall (978-1-63118-320-1)

The Philosophy of Masonry in Five Parts by Roscoe Pound
(978-1-63118-004-0)

Rosicrucian and Masonic Origins by Manly P. Hall
(978-1-63118-000-2)

The Doorway of Freemasonry and the Mason's Apron by William Harvey
(978-1-63118-001-9)

The Hiramic Legend and the Ashmolean Theory by W. B. Hextall
(978-1-63118-002-6)

A Collection of Writings Related to Occult, Esoteric, Rosicrucian and Hermetic Literature, Including Freemasonry, the Kabbalah, the Tarot, Alchemy and Theosophy various authors *Volumes 1-4*
(978-1-63118-713-1) (978-1-63118-714-8)
(978-1-63118-715-5) (978-1-63118-716-2)

Audio Versions are also Available on Audible and iTunes

Table of Contents

Introduction...7

The Story of Hiram Abiff by William Harvey...9

The Legend of Hiram Abiff by Manly P. Hall...25

The Hiramic Legend by Albert G. Mackey...47

Introduction

From the beginning of Modern Freemasonry's birthdate of 1717, the intelligentsia of humanity have found refuge for safe reflection within the walls of the fraternity. Masonic writers have produced a nearly incalculable amount of written musings on a multitude of esoteric and philosophical subjects, as they relate to the ancient mysteries that Freemasonry currently storehouses. Sadly, most of it appears to have sat largely unread, as American Freemasonry in particular, continues to transform itself into something that bares little resemblance to what it was originally designed to be. The true essence of Freemasonry is not that of blind patriotism or a single-minded national religion but one of Universal Brotherhood and altruism, designed for the betterment not just of its members but of society as a whole. In particular, for those who are not members of the fraternity, as Freemasonry has always acted as a beacon, to help guide humanity through darker times, with the hopes that one day we will collectively reach a truly enlightened age.

It's not uncommon for new members joining the fraternity to find little education within the walls of many modern lodges, in spite of so much written material available to the membership. Many older members are not simply uneducated with regards to real Masonic history and symbology, not to mention the vast arena of related subjects, but they are disinterested in all of it, as well.

Lamp of Trismegistus offers its readers highlights of Masonic study, culled from a variety of authors and viewpoints, with the hope bringing education back into the fraternity. So, be sure to check out other titles in our *Foundations of Freemasonry Series* as well as our *Esoteric Classics, Christian Apocrypha Series* and our *Theosophical Classics*, and don't be afraid to let a little altruism into your own heart or even into your Lodge.

The Story of Hiram Abiff

By William Harvey

The outstanding figure in modern Freemasonry is undoubtedly the widow's son, who is known to members of the Fraternity under the somewhat obscure name of Hiram Abiff. He dominates Craft Masonry and this, in spite of the fact that neither the Entered Apprentice nor the Fellow-Craft knows anything at all about him. It is true that, when the Master Mason recites what is called "the first part of the traditional history" to the Fellow-Craft, who is on his way to the secrets of the third degree, he pays the Fellow-Craft the compliment of saying, "*as you are doubtless aware.*" Hiram was the principal architect at the building of King Solomon's Temple, but if the Fellow-Craft is so informed, he must have acquired the knowledge altogether apart from Freemasonry as, up to that particular moment, no glimpse of the widow's son has been obtained in all the ceremonial of the First and Second Degrees. From that point onwards, however, he is chief actor in the drama, and the legend of Hiram is the most characteristic part in the ritual of the Order.

Hiram, like many other notable men in the history of the world, was distinguished in the manner of his death as was set forth in the legend, and the dramatic circumstances attending the tragedy are what give amplitude to his biography. Beyond the time, place, and means of his murder, Freemasonry knows little about the man; nor, apart from Freemasonry, are many particulars to be gleaned. All that is known of him is contained in the Volume of the Sacred Law, and even then, there is confusion, and one statement that in the opinion of Bro. Robert Freke Gould stamps the Masonic legend as a myth.

According to the author of the Second Book of Chronicles (*Chap. ii.*) Solomon sent messengers to Hiram, King of Tyre, to acquaint that friendly sovereign with the fact that he contemplated erecting a Temple, and inviting him to furnish men and materials for the prosecution of the work. Solomon's first demand was for a specially gifted craftsman.

"*Send me now,*" he says, "*a man cunning to work in gold, and in silver, and in brass, and in iron, and in purple, and crimson, and blue, and that can skill to grave with the cunning men that are with me in Judah, and in Jerusalem.*"

The King of Tyre received the embassy with cordiality, and returned a favorable answer to Solomon.

"*I have sent a cunning man,*" he says, "*endued with understanding. . . The son of a woman of the daughters of Dan, and his father was 'a man of Tyre'.*"

The account given in the First Book of the Kings (*Chap. VII.*) differs somewhat so far as the parentage of the man is concerned. There it is stated that he was "*a widow's son of the tribe of Naphtali.*" The author or editor of Kings agrees with the Chronicler that Hiram's father was a Tyrian, adding that he was "*a worker in brass.*" Josephus describes him as of Naphtali on his mother's side, his father being Ur of the stock of Israel. It is not easy to reconcile these differences. One Biblical student, Giesebrecht, suggests that the dislike felt by the editor of Kings to the idea of the Temple being built by a half-Phoenician caused him to insert the words "*a widow of the tribe of Naphtali*," the alteration of the phrase "*of the daughters of Dan*" into "*of the tribe of Naphtali*," being the more permissible, since Dan lay in the territory of Naphtali.

The clear points that emerge are that Hiram was of mixed race, the son of a brass-worker, and a man so high in his profession as to have secured the patronage of his King, and to have been deemed worthy to uphold the reputation of his country. His exalted position is inferred from the description given by the author of the Chronicles who alludes to him as "Hiram Abi," and the word "Abi," meaning "my father," is usually taken in the sense of "master," a title of respect and distinction.

The name is undoubtedly Phoenician, but there is some confusion, as to its actual form. "Hiram" is the more common rendering, but the author of the Chronicles adheres to the spelling "Huram," and other writers adopt the variant "Hirom." Mr J. F. Stenning says that it is equivalent to "Ahiram," and means "the exalted one." According to Movers, Hiram or Huram, is the name of a diety, and means "the coiled or twisted one," but other scholars regard this derivation as very improbable.

Whatever his real parentage, and whatever the exact meaning of his name, the widow's son of Freemasonry reached

Jerusalem and was thereafter intimately identified with the building of the Temple. What exact share did he have in that great work?

The editors of "The Jewish Encyclopedia" point out that there is an essential difference with regards to the nature of his technical specialty between the account preserved in the First Book of Kings and that in the Second Book of Chronicles. According to the former, Hiram was an artificer only in brass, and the pieces which he executed for the Temple were the two pillars, *Jachin* and *Boaz*, the molten sea with its twelve oxen, the ten layers with their bases, the shovels and basins, all of brass. But in the Second Book of the Chronicles he is depicted as a man of many parts, and the impression is conveyed that he superintended all the work of the Temple. Josephus seeks to reconcile the two accounts by saying that Hiram was an expert in all sorts of work, but that his chief skill lay in working in gold, silver and brass.

And there our exact knowledge of Hiram ends. History knows nothing of him. The volume of the Sacred Law is silent as to his fate. Brother Robert Freke Gould, founding on the eleventh verse of the fourth chapter of the Second Book of the Chronicles, says he "*was certainly alive at the completion of the Temple.*"

Out of this slender basis of fact Freemasonry has created a wonderfully vivid character. The Order maintains that he was the chief architect at the construction of the Temple and associates him with Hiram, King of Tyre, and Solomon, King of Israel, on a footing of Masonic equality. It suggests that these three were the most exalted personages in the Masonic world and that the secrets of a Master Mason had either descended to them, or been invented by them, and could not be communicated to anyone else without the consent of all three. There were Master Masons in abundance at the Temple, but apparently none of them had been admitted to a knowledge of the secrets and mysteries of the High and Sublime Degree. Consequently, when certain curious Fellow-Crafts sought to obtain the hidden knowledge, they were compelled to approach one or another of the three grand masters. They selected Hiram and when he refused their request they murdered him in the manner described in Masonic ritual.

"Taken literally," says Charles William Heckethorn in *The Secret Societies of all Ages and Countries,* "*the story of Hiram offers nothing so extraordinary as to deserve to be commemorated after three thousand years throughout the world by solemn rites and ceremonies. The death of an architect is not so important a matter to have more honor paid to it than is shown the memory of so many philosophers and learned men who have lost their lives in the cause of human progress . . . The legend is purely allegorical. . . The dramatic portion of the mysteries of antiquity is always sustained by a pity or man who perishes as the victim of an evil power, and rises again into a more glorious existence. In the ancient mysteries, we constantly meet with the record of a sad event, a crime which plunges nations into strife and grief, succeeded by joy and exultation.*"

Leaving for the moment the question as to the meaning of the allegory and whence it was borrowed, let us consider at what date the legend of Hiram was engrafted upon Craft Masonry.

It is generally admitted by students that the elaborate ceremonial, and multiplicity of degrees which flourish today under the general terms of Freemasonry, are of comparatively modern growth, and that before the era of Grand Lodges not more than one, or at most, two degrees were in existence. The Freemasonry of today appears to owe a good deal to the enthusiasm and imagination of two brethren who were active in the first half of the eighteenth century. These were Dr, James Anderson, an Aberdonian, who was a Presbyterian minister in London, and Dr John Theophilus Desaguliers, a native of La Rochelle, an Episcopalian clergyman, who also labored in the Metropolis. Dr George Aliver, another parson who, was keenly interested in the Craft, and contributed much to masonic literature, says that "*the name of the individual who attached the aphanism of H.A.B. to Freemasonry has never been clearly ascertained; although it may be fairly presumed that Brothers Desaguliers and Anderson were prominent parties to it,*" adding that when "*these two Brothers were publicly accused by their seceding contemporaries of manufacturing the degree,*" they "*never denied*" it. Brother Robert Freke Gould, noticing the statement of Oliver, says that Anderson and Desaguliers had been many years in their graves when the accusation was made, and that, consequently, their silence "*is not to be wondered at.*" But if Gould himself does not lay the blame or credit of the Third Degree at the door of these Brethren he favors the view that Hiram became a prominent character in Masonic ritual during the years of their activity.

"When the legend of Hiram's death was first incorporated with our older traditions, it is not easy to decide," he says, *"but in my judgment it must have taken place between 1723 and 1729, and,"* he adds, *"I should be inclined to name 1725 as the most likely year for its introduction."*

Gould is led to this view from two considerations: first, the remarkable paucity of references to Hiram in the Old Charges and early catechisms of Freemasonry, and, secondly, the prominence given to him in the edition of Dr Anderson's "Constitutions," published in 1738. He thinks, wisely, most people will agree, that if the murder of Hiram Abiff had been a tradition of the Craft in early days, not only would allusions to him be found in the literature of the Order, but he would have appeared in the earlier degrees, and not been thrust without any sort of warning into the third degree, much to the surprise of all who regard Craft Masonry as a gradually developing spectacle. As Palgrave says, *"It is not well for the personages of the historical drama to rise on the stage through the trap-doors. They should first appear entering in between the side scenes. Their play will be better understood then. We are puzzled when a king, or count, suddenly lands upon our historical ground, like a collier winched up through a shaft."*

It is not improbable, that just about the time mentioned by Gould - the close of the first quarter of the eighteenth century - the traditional history was enlarged, the ceremonial rearranged, and what was formerly the second degree expanded and then divided so as to form the degrees of Fellow-Craft *and* Master Mason. Countenance to this view by a comparison of the first and second editions of Anderson's "Constitutions." In the earliest editions, issued in 1723, the author dwells at some length upon the magnificence of King Solomon's Temple. This is repeated in the later edition, published in 1738, but a number, of details as to the manner of its erection are given which suggests that it had grown in Masonic ceremonial importance during the intervening years. For example, Anderson states that after "*the Cape-stone was celebrated by the Fraternity, their joy was soon interrupted by the sudden death of their dear master, Hiram Abiff, whom they decently interred in the Lodge near the Temple, according to ancient usage.*"

If it be assumed that the third degree was invented about 1725, and that the invention involved the introduction of the Hiramic legend, the next point for consideration is, to what source did the founders turn for material? Beyond casual references to him, the Old Charges are silent concerning Hiram, and there is nothing to indicate that he was commemorated in any way. He is simply referred to as a "Master of Geometry, " and the chief of all the various classes of workmen engaged in the building of the Temple. He appears to have been slightly more prominent in the ceremonial of the Rosicrucians with whom Freemasons are sometimes identified. Professor Buhle, in his *Historico-Critical Enquiry into the Origin of the Rosicrucians and Freemasons*, says:

> "*The building of Solomon's Temple had an obvious meaning as a prefiguration of Christianity. Hiram, simply the architect of this temple to the real professors of the art of building, was to the English Rosicrucians a type of Christ: and the legend of Masons, which represented this Hiram as having been murdered by his fellow-workmen, made the type still more striking.*"

In a footnote to his Essay, Buhle explains that "Hiram" was understood by the older Freemasons as an anagram H.I.R.A.M. derived from two Latin phrases: the one, "*Homo Jesus Redemptor AnimaruM*," and the other, "*Homo Iesus Rex Altissimus Mundi*" by "older Freemasons." Ruble probably means Rosicrucians, as phrases relating to Jesus seem singularly out of place in the plan of Craft Masonry.

If the inventors of the third degree got the suggestion from the Rosicrucian's to make Hiram the central figure in their new scheme, it is very obvious that they found their details as to his murder in "The Legend of the Temple," and turned that story to suit the purpose they had in view. The Legend is given at length in Charles William Heckethorn's singularly attractive work, *The Secret Societies of all Ages and Countries*, from which it may be summarized as follows:

> "*Hiram, the descendent of Tubal-Cain, who first constructed a furnace and worked in metals, erected a marvelous building, the Temple of Solomon, raised the golden throne of Solomon, and built many glorious edifices. But, melancholy amidst all his greatness, he lived alone, understood and loved by few, hated by many, including Solomon, who was envious of his genius and glory. When Balkis, the Queen of Sheba, came to Jerusalem, Solomon led her to behold the Temple, and the Queen was lost in admiration. The King, captivated by her beauty, offered his hand, which she accepted. On again visiting the Temple she repeatedly desired to see the architect. Solomon delayed as long as possible, but at last was forced to present Hiram Abiff to the Queen. When she wished to see the*

countless host of workmen that wrought at the Temple, Solomon protested the impossibility of assembling them all at once; but, Hiram, leaping on a stone to be better seen, with his right hand described in the air the symbolical Tau, and immediately the men hastened from all parts of the work into the presence of their master. At this the Queen wondered greatly, and secretly repented of the promise she had given the King, for she felt herself in love with the mighty architect. Solomon set himself to destroy this affection, and to prepare his rival's humiliation and ruin. For this purpose he employed three fellow-crafts, envious of Hiram, because he had refused to raise them to the degree of masters on account of their want of knowledge and their idleness. The black envy these three projected that the casting of the brazen sea, which was to raise the glory of Hiram its utmost height, should turn out a failure. The day for the casting arrived and the Queen Sheba was present. The doors that restrained the molten metal were opened, and torrents of liquid fire poured into the cast mold, wherein the brazen sea was to assume its form. But the burning mass flowed like lava over the adjacent aces. The terrified crowd fled from the advancing stream of fire, while Hiram, calm, like a god, endeavored to arrest its advance with ponderous columns of water, but without success.

"The dishonored artificer could not with draw himself from the scene of his discomfiture. Suddenly he heard a strange voice coming from above and crying, 'Hiram, Hiram, Hiram;' He raised his eyes and beheld a gigantic human figure. The apparition continued, `Come, my son, be without fear, I have rendered thee incombustible, cast thyself into the flames.' Hiram threw himself into the furnace, and where others would have found death, he tasted ineffable delights nor could he, drawn by an irresistible force, leave it, and

asked him that drew him into the abyss, `Who art thou?' `I am the father of thy fathers,' was the answer, `I am Tubal-Cain.'

"Tubal-Cain introduced Hiram into the sanctuary of fire, and into the presence of Cain, the author of his race. When Hiram was about to be restored to earth, Tubal-Cain gave him the hammer with which he himself had wrought great things, and said to him, `Thanks to this hammer and the help of the genii of fire, thou shalt speedily accomplish the work left unfinished through man's stupidity and malignity.' Hiram did not hesitate to test the wonderful efficacy of the precious instrument, and the dawn saw the great mass of bronze cast. The artist felt the most lively joy. The Queen exulted.

"One day after this, the Queen, accompanied by her maids, went beyond Jerusalem, and there encountered Hiram, alone and thoughtful. They mutually confessed their love. Solomon now hinted to the fellow-crafts that the removal of his rival, who refused to give them the master's word, would be acceptable unto himself; so when the architect came into the temple he was assailed and slain by them. They wrapped up his body, carried it to a solitary hill and buried it, planting over the grave a sprig of acacia.

"Hiram, not having made his appearance for seven days, Solomon, to satisfy the clamor of the people, was forced to have him searched for. The body was found by three masters, and they, suspecting that he had been slain by the three fellow-crafts for refusing them the master's word, determined nevertheless for greater security to change the word. The three fellow-crafts were traced, but *rather than fall into the hands of their pursuers, they committed suicide, and their heads were brought to Solomon."*

Based as it obviously was on this legend of the Temple, the question still remains, why was the story of the death of Hiram engrafted with so much detail upon Freemasonry? The postulant is taught that the peculiar object of the Third Degree is to teach the heart to seek for happiness in the consciousness of a life well-spent, and invited to reflect upon death and to realize that to the just and virtuous man death has no terrors equal to the stain of falsehood and dishonor. All excellent moral teaching, but not illustrated in any way by the career of Hiram Abiff, concerning whose life and conduct we know absolutely nothing. And it seems that we must look for an explanation in some other direction.

Many writers - chiefly non-Masons - have sought to throw light upon the subject, and with one voice they agree that the story of the death of Hiram is simply the Masonic way of serving up an ancient mystery. Mr John Fellows, who brings a mass of knowledge to a study of the subject, says that:

"the story of Hiram is only another version, like those of Adonis and Astarte, and of Ceres and Prosperpina, of the fable of Osiris and Isis. The likeness throughout," he adds, *"is so exact as not to admit of doubt. The search for the body of Hiram; the enquiries made of a wayfaring man, and the intelligence received; the sitting down of one of the party to rest and refresh himself, and the hint conveyed by the sprig over the grave; the body of Hiram remaining fourteen days in the grave prepared by the assassins before it was*

discovered, all have allusion to, and comport with, the allegory of Osiris and Isis. The condition even in which the grave of Hiram is found, covered with green moss and turf, corresponds very much with that in which Isis found the coffin of Osiris."

Assuming that Mr Fellows and those who agree with him are correct, what is the reason why the inventors of the Third Degree in the first quarter of the eighteenth century gave a Biblical turn to an old-world fable and introduced it into Freemasonry to teach the doctrine of the resurrection of the dead? The question is not easy to answer, and at most one can but hazard a guess.

May it not be that those who were anxious to build up the degree found their starting point in the anagram familiar to the Rosicrucian's which, by a very striking coincidence, agreed with the name of the principal architect of the Temple? Thus directed to Hiram they, decided to turn that craftsman to account and found much material ready to their hands in the Legend of the Temple. But the love story of the Queen of Sheba and the jealousy of Solomon were of no dramatic value to them in developing the degree, and consequently they had to adapt the story to their particular needs. What the ultimate origin of Freemasonry was may never be discovered, but much of the elaborate ceremonial has a close affinity to early sun-worship and where, therefore, would the Authors more readily turn than to one of the solar myths. In the legend of Osiris they found something that fitted in exactly with their scheme, and just as the H.I.R.A.M. of the Rosicrucian's referred to that Son of God who is the Light of the World, so their Hiram was made to represent Osiris, or the sun, the glorious luminary of the day. The three fellow-crafts, as the ceremonial of the degree takes form, are stationed at the west, south and east entrances, and these are regions illuminated by the Sun. Twelve persons play an important part in the tragedy; the number, no doubt, alludes to the twelve signs of the Zodiac, and it has been suggested that the three assassins symbolize the three inferior signs of winter, Libra, Scorpio, and Sagittarius. The Sun descends in the west, and it is at the west door that Hiram is slain. The acacia which typifies the new vegetation, that will come as "a result of the Sun's resurrection," and is found in many ancient solar allegories, and is therefore quite naturally introduced into the Masonic story. According to one statement, Hiram's body is found in a state of decay, having lain fourteen days; the body of Osiris was cut into fourteen pieces. Another statement insists that the body was found on the seventh day, and this again may allude to the resurrection of the Sun, "*which actually takes place in the seventh month after his passage through the inferior signs, that passage which is called his descent into hell.*" Other details in the Masonic tragedy are related to the solar myth. It is through the instrumentality of Leo - the Lion - that Osiris is raised, for when he re-enters that sign, he regains his former strength. Hiram was raised by the Lion's grip, and it is by that grip that the Freemason is raised from a figurative death to a reunion with the companions of his former toil. The parallel is wonderfully complete.

An early catechism of the Craft says that Masonry is "*a system of morality, veiled in allegory, and illustrated by symbols.*" Today it is something more. The First Degree accords with the definition; but the second degree is largely concerned with the erection of a Temple to the Lord, and, the Third Degree points the Craftsman to the Grand Lodge above to which he may hope to ascend after he has passed through the valley of the shadow of death. All this is religion - not morals; and it is as part of our common faith in immortality that Hiram's death is used as an illustration in the high and sublime degree. Just as in early pagan belief, the Sun was supposed to lose his strength in the dark days of winter, and rise again to glory in the height of summer tide; and just as, in the ceremonial of the Rosicrucians, the Son of Man, who was slain had a glorious resurrection to eternal life, so, throughout all the world, wherever Craft Masonry is practiced, the postulant typifies our Master Hiram, not alone to show that death is preferable to dishonor, but to impress upon the Fraternity that the just and virtuous man may hope to be received as a worthy brother into the Grand Lodge above, where the world's Great Architect rules and reigns forever.

The Legend of Hiram Abiff
By Manly P. Hall

When Solomon--the beloved of God, builder of the Everlasting House, and Grand Master of the Lodge of Jerusalem--ascended the throne of his father David he consecrated his life to the erection of a temple to God and a palace for the kings of Israel. David's faithful friend, Hiram, King of Tyre, hearing that a son of David sat upon the throne of Israel, sent messages of congratulation and offers of assistance to the new ruler. In his *History of the Jews,* Josephus mentions that copies of the letters passing between the two kings were then to be seen both at Jerusalem and at Tyre. Despite Hiram's lack of appreciation for the twenty cities of Galilee which Solomon presented to him upon the completion of the temple, the two monarchs remained the best of friends. Both were famous for their wit and wisdom, and when they exchanged letters each devised puzzling questions to test the mental ingenuity of the other. Solomon made an agreement with Hiram of Tyre promising vast amounts of barley, wheat, corn, wine, and oil as wages for the masons and carpenters from Tyre who were to assist the Jews in the erection of the temple. Hiram also supplied cedars and other fine trees, which were made into rafts and floated down the sea to Joppa, whence they were taken inland by Solomon's workmen to the temple site.

Because of his great love for Solomon, Hiram of Tyre sent also the Grand Master of the Dionysiac Architects, Hiram

Abiff, a Widow's Son, who had no equal among the craftsmen of the earth. Hiram is described as being "a Tyrian by birch, but of Israelitish descent," and "a second Bezaleel, honored by his king with the title of Father." *The Freemason's Pocket Companion* (published in 1771) describes Hiram as "the most cunning, skillful and curious workman that ever lived, whose abilities were not confined to building alone, but extended to all kinds of work, whether in gold, silver, brass or iron; whether in linen, tapestry, or embroidery; whether considered as an architect, statuary [sic]; founder or designer, separately or together, he equally excelled. From his designs, and under his direction, all the rich and splendid furniture of the Temple and its several appendages were begun, carried on, and finished. Solomon appointed him, in his absence, to fill the chair, as Deputy Grand-Master; and in his presence, Senior Grand-Warden, Master of work, and general overseer of all artists, as well those whom David had formerly procured from Tyre and Sidon, as those Hiram should now send."

Although an immense amount of labor was involved in its construction, Solomon's Temple--in the words of George Oliver--"was *only a small building and very inferior in point of size to some of our churches.*" The number of buildings contiguous to it and the vast treasure of gold and precious stones used in its construction concentrated a great amount of wealth within the temple area. In the midst of the temple stood the Holy of Holies, sometimes called the Oracle. It was an exact cube, each dimension being twenty cubits, and exemplified the influence of Egyptian symbolism. The buildings of the temple group were ornamented with 1,453 columns of Parian marble, magnificently sculptured, and 2,906 pilasters decorated with capitals. There was a broad porch facing the east, and the *sanctum sanctorum* was upon the west. According to tradition, the various buildings and courtyards could hold in all 300,000 persons. Both the Sanctuary and the Holy of Holies were entirely lined with solid gold plates encrusted with jewels.

King Solomon began the building of the temple in the fourth year of his reign on what would be, according to modern calculation, the 21st day of April, and finished it in the eleventh year of his reign on the 23rd day of October. The temple was begun in the 480th year after the children of Israel had passed the Red Sea. Part of the labor of construction included the building of an artificial foundation on the brow of Mount Moriah. The stones for the temple were hoisted from quarries directly beneath Mount Moriah and were trued before being brought to the surface. The brass and golden ornaments for the temple were cast in molds in the clay ground between Succoth and Zeredatha, and the wooden parts were all finished before they reached the temple site. The building was put together, consequently, without sound and without instruments, all its parts fitting exactly

> "without *the hammer of contention, the axe of division, or any tool of mischief.*"

Anderson's much-discussed *Constitutions of the Free-Masons*, published in London in 1723, and reprinted by Benjamin Franklin in Philadelphia in 1734, thus describes the division of the laborers engaged in the building of the Everlasting House:

"But Dagon's Temple, and the finest structures of Tyre and Sidon, could not be compared with the Eternal God's Temple at Jerusalem, ...there were employed about it no less than 3,600 Princes, or Master-Masons, to conduct the work according to Solomon's directions, with 80,000 hewers of stone in the mountain, or Fellow Craftsmen, and 70,000 labourers, in all 153,600 besides the levy under Adoniram to work in the mountains of Lebanon by turns with the Sidonians, viz., 30,000, being in all 183,600."

Daniel Sickels gives 3,300 overseers, instead of 3,600, and lists the three Grand Masters separately. The same author estimates the cost of the temple at nearly four thousand millions of dollars.

The Masonic legend of the building of Solomon's Temple does not in every particular parallel the Scriptural version, especially in those portions relating to Hiram Abiff. According to the Biblical account, this Master workman returned to his own country; in the Masonic allegory he is foully murdered. On this point A. E. Waite, in his *New Encyclopædia of Freemasonry,* makes the following explanatory comment:

"The legend of the Master-Builder is the great allegory of Masonry. It happens that his figurative story is grounded on the fact of a personality mentioned in Holy Scripture, but this historical background is of the accidents and not the essence; the significance is in the allegory and not in any point of history which may lie behind it."

Hiram, as Master of the Builders, divided his workmen into three groups, which were termed Entered Apprentices, Fellow-Craftsmen, and Master Masons. To each division he gave certain passwords and signs by which their respective excellence could be quickly determined. While all were classified according to their merits some were dissatisfied, for they desired a more exalted position than they were capable of filling. At last three Fellow-Craftsmen, more daring than their companions, determined to force Hiram to reveal to them the password of the Master's degree. Knowing that Hiram always went into the unfinished *sanctum sanctorum* at high noon to pray, these *ruffians--whose* names were Jubela, Jubelo, and Jubelum-- lay in wait for him, one at each of the main gates of the temple. Hiram, about to leave the temple by the south gate, was suddenly confronted by Jubela armed with a twenty-four-inch gauge. Upon Hiram's refusal to reveal the Master's *Word,* the ruffian struck him on the throat with the rule, and the wounded Master then hastened to the west gate, where Jubelo, armed with a square, awaited him and made a similar demand. Again Hiram was silent, and the second assassin struck him on the breast with the square. Hiram thereupon staggered to the east gate, only to be met there by Jubelum armed with a maul. When Hiram, refused him the Master's Word, Jubelum struck the Master between the eyes with the mallet and Hiram fell dead.

The body of Hiram was buried by the murderers over the brow of Mount Moriah and a sprig of acacia placed upon the grave. The murderers then sought to escape punishment for their crime by embarking for Ethiopia, but the port was closed. All three were finally captured, and after admitting their guilt were duly executed. Parties of three were then sent out by King Solomon, and one of these groups discovered the newly made grave marked by the evergreen sprig. After the Entered Apprentices and the Fellow- Craftsmen had failed to resurrect their Master from the dead he was finally *raised* by the Master Mason with the "strong *grip of a Lion's Paw.*"

To the initiated Builder the name *Hiram Abiff* signifies "My Father, the Universal Spirit, one in essence, three in aspect." Thus the murdered Master is a type of the Cosmic Martyr--the crucified Spirit of Good, the *dying god--whose* Mystery is celebrated throughout the world. Among the manuscripts of Dr. Sigismund Bastrom, the initiated Rosicrucian, appears the following extract from von Welling concerning the true philosophic nature of the Masonic Hiram:

> "The original word [Cheth-Yod-Resh-Mem], Hiram, is a radical word consisting of three consonants *Cheth, Resh* and *Mem*. (1) *Cheth,* signifies *Chamah,* the Sun's light, i. e. the *Universal, invisible, cold fire of Nature* attracted by the Sun, manifested into *light* and sent down to us and to every planetary body belonging to the solar system. (2) *Resh,* signifies *Ruach,* i. e. *Spirit, air, wind,* as being the Vehicle which conveys and collects the light into numberless Foci, wherein the solar rays of light are agitated by a circular motion and manifested in *Heat* and *burning Fire*. (3) *Mem,* signifies *majim, water, humidity,* but rather the *mother of water,* i. e. Radical Humidity or a particular kind of condensed air. These three constitute the Universal Agent or fire of Nature in one word, [Cheth-Yod-Resh-Mem], *CHiram,* not Hiram."

Albert Pike mentions several forms of the name *CHiram: Khirm, Khurm,* and *Khur-Om,* the latter ending in the sacred Hindu monosyllable *OM,* which may also be extracted from the names of the three murderers. Pike further relates the three ruffians to a triad of stars in the constellation of Libra and also calls attention to the fact that the Chaldean god Bal--metamorphosed into a demon by the Jews--appears in the name of each of the murderers, Jubela, Jubelo, and Jubelum. To interpret the Hiramic legend requires familiarity with both the Pythagorean and Qabbalistic systems of numbers and letters, and also the philosophic and astronomic cycles of the Egyptians, Chaldeans, and Brahmins. For example, consider the number 33. The first temple of Solomon stood for thirty-three years in its pristine splendor. At the end of that time it was pillaged by the Egyptian King Shishak, and finally in 588 B.C., it was completely destroyed by Nebuchadnezzar and the people of Jerusalem were led into captivity to Babylon. (See *General History of Freemasonry,* by Robert Macoy.) Also King David ruled for thirty- three years in Jerusalem; the Masonic Order is divided into thirty-three symbolic degrees; there are thirty-three segments in the human spinal column; and Jesus was crucified in the thirty-third year of His life.

The efforts made to discover the origin of the Hiramic legend show that, while the legend in its present form is comparatively modem, its underlying principles run back to remotest antiquity. It is generally admitted by modem Masonic scholars that the story of the martyred Hiram is based upon the Egyptian rites of Osiris, whose death and resurrection figuratively portrayed the spiritual death of man and his regeneration through initiation into the Mysteries. Hiram is also identified with Hermes through the inscription on the Emerald Table. From these associations it is evident that Hiram is to be considered as a prototype of humanity; in fact he is Plato's *Idea* (archetype) of man. As Adam after the Fall symbolizes the Idea of human degeneration, so Hiram through his resurrection symbolizes the Idea of human regeneration.

On the 19th day of March, 1314, Jacques de Molay, the last Grand Master of the Knights Templars, was burned on a pyre erected upon that point of the islet of the Seine, at Paris, where afterwards was erected the statue of King Henry IV. (See *The Indian Religions*, by Hargrave Jennings.) "It is mentioned as a tradition in some of the accounts of the burning," writes Jennings, "that Molay, ere he expired, summoned Clement, the Pope who had pronounced the bull of abolition against the Order and had condemned the Grand Master to the flames, to appear, within forty days, before the Supreme Eternal judge, and Philip [the king] to the same awful tribunal within the space of a year. Both predictions were fulfilled." The close relationship between Freemasonry and the original Knights Templars has caused the story of Hiram to be linked with the martyrdom of Jacques de Molay. According to this interpretation, the three *ruffians* who cruelly slew their Master at the gates of the temple because he refused to reveal the secrets of his Order represent the Pope, the king, and the executioners. De Molay died maintaining his innocence and refusing to disclose the philosophical and magical arcana of the Templars.

Those who have sought to identify Hiram with the murdered King Charles the First conceive the Hiramic legend to have been invented for that purpose by Elias Ashmole, a mystical philosopher, who was probably a member of the Rosicrucian Fraternity. Charles was dethroned in 1647 and died on the block in 1649, leaving the Royalist party leaderless. An attempt has been made to relate the term "the Sons of the Widow" (an appellation frequently applied to members of the Masonic Order) to this incident in English history, for by the murder of her king England became a *Widow* and all Englishmen *Widow's Sons*.

To the mystic Christian Mason, Hiram. represents the Christ who in three days (degrees) *raised* the temple of His body from its earthly sepulcher. His three murderers were Cæsar's agent (the state), the Sanhedrin (the church), and the incited populace (the mob). Thus considered, Hiram becomes the higher nature of man and the murderers are ignorance, superstition, and fear. The indwelling Christ can give expression to Himself in this world only through man's thoughts, feelings, and actions. Right thinking, right feeling, and right action--these are three gates through which the Christ power passes into the material world, there to labor in the erection of the Temple of Universal Brotherhood. Ignorance, superstition, and fear are three ruffians through whose agencies the Spirit of Good is murdered and a false kingdom, controlled by wrong thinking, wrong feeling, and wrong action, established in its stead. In the material universe evil appears ever victorious.

"In this sense," writes Daniel Sickels, "the myth of the Tyrian is perpetually repeated in the history of human affairs. Orpheus was murdered, and his body thrown into the Hebrus;

Socrates was made to drink the hemlock; and, in all ages, we have seen Evil temporarily triumphant, and Virtue and Truth calumniated, persecuted, crucified, and slain. But Eternal justice marches surely and swiftly through the world: the Typhons, the children of darkness, the plotters of crime, all the infinitely varied forms of evil, are swept into oblivion; and Truth and Virtue--for a time laid low--come forth, clothed with diviner majesty, and crowned with everlasting glory!" (See *General Ahiman Rezon.*)

If, as there is ample reason to suspect, the modern Freemasonic Order was profoundly influenced by, if it is not an actual outgrowth of, Francis Bacon's secret society, its symbolism is undoubtedly permeated with Bacon's two great ideals: universal education and universal democracy. The deadly enemies of universal education are ignorance, superstition, and fear, by which the human soul is held in bondage to the lowest part of its own constitution. The arrant enemies of universal democracy have ever been the crown, the tiara, and the torch. Thus Hiram symbolizes that ideal state of spiritual, intellectual, and physical emancipation which has ever been sacrificed upon the altar of human selfishness. Hiram is the Beautifier of the Eternal House. Modern utilitarianism, however, sacrifices the beautiful for the practical, in the same breath declaring the obvious lie that selfishness, hatred, and discord are practical.

Dr. Orville Ward Owen found a considerable part of the first thirty-two degrees of Freemasonic ritualism hidden in the text of the First Shakespeare Folio. Masonic emblems are to be observed also upon the title pages of nearly every book published by Bacon. Sir Francis Bacon considered himself as a living sacrifice upon the altar of human need; he was obviously *cut down* in the midst of his labors, and no student of his *New Atlantis* can fail to recognize the Masonic symbolism contained therein. According to the observations of Joseph Fort Newton, the Temple of Solomon described by Bacon in that utopian romance was not a house at all but the name of an ideal state. Is it not true that the Temple of Freemasonry is also emblematic of a condition of society? While, as before stated, the principles of the Hiramic legend are of the greatest antiquity, it is not impossible that its present form may be based upon incidents in the life of Lord Bacon, who passed through the philosophic death and was *raised* in Germany.

In an old manuscript appears the statement that the Freemasonic Order was formed by alchemists and Hermetic philosophers who had banded themselves together to protect their secrets against the infamous methods used by avaricious persons to wring from them the secret of gold-making. The fact that the Hiramic legend contains an alchemical formula gives credence to this story. Thus the building of Solomon's Temple represents the consummation of the *magnum opus,* which cannot be realized without the assistance of Hiram, the Universal Agent. The Masonic Mysteries teach the initiate how to prepare within his own soul a miraculous *powder of projection* by which it is possible for him to transmute the base lump of human ignorance, perversion, and discord into an ingot of spiritual and philosophic gold.

Sufficient similarity exists between the Masonic Hiram and the *Kundalini* of Hindu mysticism to warrant the assumption that Hiram may be considered a symbol also of the Spirit Fire moving through the sixth ventricle of the spinal column. The exact science of human regeneration is the Lost Key of Masonry, for when the Spirit Fire is *lifted up* through the thirty-three degrees, or segments of the spinal column, and enters into the domed chamber of the human skull, it finally passes into the pituitary body (Isis), where it invokes Ra (the pineal gland) and demands the Sacred Name. Operative Masonry, in the fullest meaning of that term, signifies the process by which the Eye of Horus is opened. E. A. Wallis Budge has noted that in some of the papyri illustrating the entrance of the souls of the dead into the judgment hall of Osiris the deceased person has a pine cone attached to the crown of his head. The Greek mystics also carried a symbolic staff, the upper end being in the form of a pine cone, which was called the *thyrsus* of Bacchus. In the human brain there is a tiny gland called the pineal body, which is the sacred eye of the ancients, and corresponds to the third eye of the Cyclops. Little is known concerning the function of the pineal body, which Descartes suggested (more wisely than he knew) might be the abode of the spirit of man. As its name signifies, the pineal gland is the sacred pine cone in man--the *eye single,* which cannot be opened until Hiram (the Spirit Fire) is *raised* through the sacred seals which are called the Seven Churches in Asia.

There is an Oriental painting which shows three sun bursts. One sunburst covers the head, in the midst of which sits Brahma with four heads, his body a mysterious dark color. The second sunburst--which covers the heart, solar plexus, and upper abdominal region--shows Vishnu sitting in the blossom of the lotus on a couch formed of the coils of the serpent of cosmic motion, its seven-hooded head forming a canopy over the god. The third sunburst is over the generative system, in the midst of which sits Shiva, his body a grayish white and the Ganges River flowing out of the crown of his head. This painting was the work of a Hindu mystic who spent many years subtly concealing great philosophical principles within these figures. The Christian legends could be related also to the human body by the same method as the Oriental, for the arcane meanings hidden in the teachings of both schools are identical.

As applied to Masonry, the three sunbursts represent the gates of the temple at which Hiram was struck, there being no gate in the north because the sun never shines from the northern angle of the heavens. The north is the symbol of the physical because of its relation to ice (crystallized water) and to the body (crystallized spirit). In man the light shines toward the north but never from it, because the body has no light of its own but shines with the reflected glory of the divine life-particles concealed within physical substance. For this reason the moon is accepted as the symbol of man's physical nature. Hiram is the mysterious fiery, airy water which must be raised through the three grand centers symbolized by the ladder with three rungs and the sunburst flowers mentioned in the description of the Hindu painting. It must also pass upward by means of the ladder of seven rungs-the seven plexuses proximate to the spine. The nine segments of the sacrum and coccyx are pierced by ten foramina, through which pass the roots of the Tree of Life. Nine is the sacred number of man, and in the symbolism of the sacrum and coccyx a great mystery is concealed. That part of the body from the kidneys downward was termed by the early Qabbalists the *Land of Egypt* into which the children of Israel were taken during the captivity. Out of Egypt, Moses (the illuminated mind, as his name implies) led the tribes of Israel (the twelve faculties) by *raising* the brazen serpent in the wilderness upon the symbol of the Tau cross. Not only Hiram but the god-men of nearly every pagan Mystery ritual are personifications of the Spirit Fire in the human spinal cord.

The astronomical aspect of the Hiramic legend must not be overlooked. The tragedy of Hiram is enacted annually by the sun during its passage through the signs of the zodiac.

"From the journey of the Sun through the twelve signs," writes Albert Pike, "come the legend of the twelve labors of Hercules, and the incarnations of Vishnu and Buddha. Hence came the legend of the murder of Khurum, representative of the Sun, by the three Fellow-Crafts, symbols of the Winter signs, Capricornus, Aquarius, and Pisces, who assailed him at the three gates of Heaven and slew him at the Winter Solstice. Hence the search for him by the nine Fellow-Crafts, the other nine signs, his finding, burial, and resurrection." (See *Morals and Dogma.*)

Other authors consider Libra, Scorpio, and Sagittarius as the three murderers of the sun, inasmuch as Osiris was murdered by Typhon, to whom were assigned the thirty degrees of the constellation of Scorpio. In the Christian Mysteries also Judas signifies the Scorpion, and the thirty pieces of silver for which he betrayed His Lord represent the number of degrees in that sign. Having been struck by Libra (the state), Scorpio (the church), and Sagittarius (the mob), the sun (Hiram) is secretly home through the darkness by the signs of Capricorn, Aquarius, and Pisces and buried over the brow of a hill (the vernal equinox). Capricorn has for its symbol an old man with a scythe in his hand. This is Father Time-- a wayfarer--who is symbolized in Masonry as straightening out the ringlets of a young girl's hair. If the Weeping Virgin be considered a symbol of Virgo, and Father Time with his scythe a symbol of Capricorn, then the interval of ninety degrees between these two signs will be found to correspond to that occupied by the three murderers. Esoterically, the urn containing the ashes of Hiram represents the human heart. Saturn, the old man who lives at the north pole, and brings with him to the children of men a sprig of evergreen (the Christmas tree), is familiar to the little folks under the name of *Santa Claus,* for he brings each winter the gift of a new year.

The martyred sun is discovered by Aries, a Fellow-Craftsman, and at the vernal equinox the process of raising him begins. This is finally accomplished by the Lion of Judah, who in ancient times occupied the position of the keystone of the Royal Arch of Heaven. The precession of the equinoxes causes various signs to play the role of the murderers of the sun during the different ages of the world, but the principle involved remains unchanged. Such is the cosmic story of Hiram, the Universal Benefactor, the Fiery Architect: of the Divine House, who carries with him to the grave that Lost Word which, when spoken, *raises* all life to power and glory. According to Christian mysticism, when the Lost Word is found it is discovered in a stable, surrounded by beasts and marked by a star. "After the sun leaves Leo," writes Robert Hewitt Brown, "the days begin to grow unequivocally shorter as the sun declines toward the autumnal equinox, to be again slain by the *three* autumnal months, lie dead through the *three* winter ones, and be raised again by the *three* vernal ones. Each year the great tragedy is repeated, and the glorious resurrection takes place." (See *Stellar Theology and Masonic Astronomy.*)

Hiram is termed *dead* because in the average individual the cosmic creative forces are limited in their manifestation to purely physical--and correspondingly materialistic--expression. Obsessed by his belief in the reality and permanence of physical existence, man does not correlate the material universe with the blank north wall of the temple. As the solar light symbolically is said to die as it approaches the winter solstice, so the physical world may be termed the winter solstice of the spirit. Reaching the winter solstice, the sun apparently stands still for three days and then, rolling away the stone of winter, begins its triumphal march north towards the summer solstice. The condition of ignorance may be likened to the winter solstice of philosophy; spiritual understanding to the summer solstice. From this point of view, initiation into the Mysteries becomes the vernal equinox of the spirit, at which time the Hiram in man crosses from the realm of mortality into that of eternal life. The autumnal equinox is analogous to the mythological *fall* of man, at which time the human spirit descended into the realms of Hades by being immersed in the illusion of terrestrial existence.

In *An Essay on the Beautiful,* Plotinus describes the refining effect of beauty upon the unfolding consciousness of man. Commissioned to decorate the Everlasting House, Hiram Abiff is the embodiment of the beautifying principle. Beauty is essential to the natural unfoldment of the human soul. The Mysteries held that man, in part at least, was the product of his environment. Therefore they considered it imperative that every person be surrounded by objects which would evoke the highest and noblest sentiments. They proved that it was possible to produce beauty in life by surrounding life with beauty. They discovered that symmetrical bodies were built by souls continuously in the presence of symmetrical bodies; that noble thoughts were produced by minds surrounded by examples of mental nobility. Conversely, if a man were forced to look upon an ignoble or asymmetrical structure it would arouse within him a sense of ignobility which would provoke him to commit ignoble deeds. If an ill-proportioned building were erected in the midst of a city there would be ill-proportioned children born in that community; and men and women, gazing upon the asymmetrical structure, would live inharmonious lives. Thoughtful men of antiquity realized that their great philosophers were the natural products of the æsthetic ideals of architecture, music, and art established as the standards of the cultural systems of the time.

The substitution of the discord of the fantastic for the harmony of the beautiful constitutes one of the great tragedies of every civilization. Not only were the Savior-Gods of the ancient world beautiful, but each performed a ministry of beauty, seeking to effect man's regeneration by arousing within him the love of the beautiful. A renaissance of the golden age of fable can be made possible only by the elevation of beauty to its rightful dignity as the all-pervading, idealizing quality in the religious, ethical, sociological, scientific, and political departments of life. The Dionysiac Architects were consecrated to the *raising* of their Master Spirit--Cosmic Beauty--from the sepulcher of material ignorance and selfishness by erecting buildings which were such perfect exemplars of symmetry and majesty that they were actually magical formulæ by which was evoked the spirit of the martyred Beautifier entombed within a materialistic world.

In the Masonic Mysteries the triune spirit of man (the light Delta) is symbolized by the three Grand Masters of the Lodge of Jerusalem. As God is the pervading principle of three worlds, in each of which He manifests as an active principle, so the spirit of man, partaking of the nature of Divinity, dwells upon three planes of being: the Supreme, the Superior, and the Inferior spheres of the Pythagoreans. At the gate of the Inferior sphere (the underworld, or dwelling place of mortal creatures) stands the guardian of Hades--the three--headed dog Cerberus, who is analogous to the three murderers of the Hiramic legend. According to this symbolic interpretation of the triune spirit, Hiram is the third, or incarnating, part-- the Master Builder who through all ages erects living temples of flesh and blood as shrines of the Most High. Hiram comes forth as a flower and is cut down; he *dies* at the gates of matter; he is *buried* in the elements of creation, but--like Thor--he swings his mighty hammer in the fields of space, sets the primordial atoms in motion, and establishes order out of Chaos. As the potentiality of cosmic power within each human soul, Hiram lies waiting for man by the elaborate ritualism of life to transmute potentiality into divine potency. As the sense perceptions of the individual increase, however, man gains ever greater control over his various parts, and the spirit of life within gradually attains freedom. The three murderers represent the laws of the Inferior world-- birth, growth, and decay--which ever frustrate the plan of the Builder. To the average individual, physical birch actually signifies the death of Hiram, and physical death the resurrection of Hiram. To the initiate, however, the resurrection of the spiritual nature is accomplished without the intervention of physical death.

The curious symbols found in the base of Cleopatra's Needle now standing in Central Park, New York, were interpreted as being of first Masonic significance by S. A. Zola, 33° Past Grand Master of the Grand Lodge of Egypt. Masons' marks and symbols are to be found on the stones of numerous public buildings not only in England and on the Continent but also in Asia. In his *Indian Masons' Marks of the Moghul Dynasty,* A. Gorham describes scores of markings appearing on the walls of buildings such as the *Taj Mahal,* the *Jama Masjid,* and that: famous Masonic structure, the *Kutab Minar.* According to those who regard Masonry as an outgrowth of the secret society of architects and builders which for thousands of years formed a caste of master craftsmen, Hiram Abiff was the Tyrian Grand Master of a world-wide organization of artisans, with headquarters in Tyre. Their philosophy consisted of incorporating into the measurements and ornamentation of temples, palaces, mausoleums, fortresses, and other public buildings their knowledge of the laws controlling the universe. Every initiated workman was given a hieroglyphic with which he marked the stones he trued to show to all posterity that he thus dedicated to the Supreme Architect of the Universe each perfected product of his labor. Concerning Masons' marks, Robert Freke Gould writes:

> "It is very remarkable that these marks are to be found in all countries--in the chambers of the Great Pyramid at Gizeh, on the underground walls of Jerusalem, in Herculaneum and Pompeii, on Roman walls and Grecian temples, in Hindustan, Mexico, Peru, Asia Minor--as well as on the great ruins of England, France, Germany, Scotland, Italy, Portugal and Spain." (See *A Concise History of Freemasonry.*)

From this viewpoint the story of Hiram may well represent the incorporation of the divine secrets of architecture into the actual parts and dimensions of earthly buildings. The three degrees of the Craft bury the Grand Master (the Great Arcanum) in the actual structure they erect, after first having *killed* him with the builders' tools, by reducing the dimensionless Spirit of Cosmic Beauty to the limitations of concrete form. These abstract ideals of architecture can be resurrected, however, by the Master Mason who, by meditating upon the structure, releases therefrom the divine principles of architectonic philosophy incorporated or *buried* within it. Thus the physical building is actually the tomb or embodiment of the Creative Ideal of which its material dimensions are but the shadow.

Moreover, the Hiramic legend may be considered to embody the vicissitudes of philosophy itself. As institutions for the dissemination of ethical culture, the pagan Mysteries were the architects of civilization. Their power and dignity were personified in Hiram Abiff--the Master Builder--but they eventually fell a victim to the onslaughts of that recurrent trio of state, church, and mob. They were desecrated by the state, jealous of their wealth and power; by the early church, fearful of their wisdom; and by the rabble or soldiery incited by both state and church. As Hiram when *raised* from his grave whispers the Master Mason's Word which was lost through his untimely death, so according to the tenets of philosophy the reestablishment or resurrection of the ancient Mysteries will result in the rediscovery of that secret teaching without which civilization must continue in a state of spiritual confusion and uncertainty.

When the mob governs, man is ruled by ignorance; when the church governs, he is ruled by superstition; and when the state governs, he is ruled by fear. Before men can live together in harmony and understanding, ignorance must be transmuted into wisdom, superstition into an illumined faith, and fear into love. Despite statements to the contrary, Masonry is a religion seeking to unite God and man by elevating its initiates to that level of consciousness whereon they can behold with clarified vision the workings of the Great Architect of the Universe. From age to age the vision of a perfect civilization is preserved as the ideal for mankind. In the midst of that civilization shall stand a mighty university wherein both the sacred and secular sciences concerning the mysteries of life will be freely taught to all who will assume the philosophic life. Here creed and dogma will have no place; the superficial will be removed and only the essential be preserved. The world will be ruled by its most illumined minds, and each will occupy the position for which he is most admirably fitted.

The great university will be divided into grades, admission to which will be through preliminary tests or initiations. Here mankind will be instructed in the most sacred, the most secret, and the most enduring of all Mysteries-- Symbolism. Here the initiate will be taught that every visible object, every abstract thought, every emotional reaction is but the symbol of an eternal principle. Here mankind will learn that Hiram (Truth) lies buried in every atom of Kosmos; that every form is a symbol and every symbol the tomb of an eternal verity. Through education-- spiritual, mental, moral, and physical--man will learn to release living truths from their lifeless coverings. The perfect government of the earth must be patterned eventually after that divine government by which the universe is ordered. In that day when perfect order is reestablished, with peace universal and good triumphant, men will no longer seek for happiness, for they shall find it welling up within themselves. Dead hopes, dead aspirations, dead virtues shall rise from their graves, and the Spirit of Beauty and Goodness repeatedly slain by ignorant men shall again be the Master of Work. Then shall sages sit upon the seats of the mighty and the gods walk with men.

The Hiramic Legend
By Albert G. Mackey

This is the most important of all the legends of Freemasonry. It will therefore be considered in respect to its origin, its history, and its meaning;

Before, however, proceeding to the discussion of these important subjects, and the investigation of the truly mythical character of Hiram Abif, it will be proper to inquire into the meaning of his name, or rather the meaning of the epithet that accompanies it. In the places in Scripture in which he is mentioned he is called at one time (in 2 Chronicles ii., 13), by the King of Tyre, in the letter written by him to King Solomon, Churam Abi; in another place (in 2 Chronicles iv., 16), where the writer of the narrative is recording the work done by him for Solomon, Churam Abiv, or, as it might be pronounced according to the sound of the Hebrew letters, Abiu. But Luther, in his German translation of the Bible, adopted the pronunciation Abif, exchanging the flat v for the sharp f. In this he was followed by Anderson, who was the first to present the full name of Hiram Abif to the Craft. This he did in the first edition of the English book of Constitutions.

And since his time at least the appellation of Hiram Abif has been adopted by and become familiar to the Craft as the name of the cunning or skillful artist who was sent by Hiram, King of Tyre, to assist King Solomon in the construction of the Temple. In Chronicles and Kings we find Churam or Huram, as we may use the initial letter as a guttural or an aspirate, and Chiram or Hiram, the vowel u or i being indifferently used. But the Masonic usage has universally adopted the word Hiram.

Now, the Abi and Abiv, used by the King of Tyre, in the book of Chronicles form no part of the name, but are simply inflections of the possessive pronouns my and his suffixed to the appellative Ab. Ab in Hebrew means father, i is my, and in, iv, or if is his. Abi is therefore my father, and so he is called by the King of Tyre when he is describing him to Solomon, " Hiram my father;" Abif is his father, and he is so spoken of by the historian when he recounts the various kinds of work which were done for King Solomon by "Hiram his father."

But the word Ab in Hebrew, though primarily signifying a male parent, has other derivative significations. It is evident that in none of the passages in which he is mentioned is it intended to intimate that he held such relationship to either the King of Tyre or the King of Israel.

The word "father" was applied by the Hebrews as a term of honor, or to signify a station of preeminence. Buxtorf says it sometimes signified Master, and he cites the fourth chapter of Genesis, where Jabal is called the father of cattle and Jubal the father of musicians.

Hiram Abif was most probably selected by the King of Tyre to be sent to Solomon as a skillful artificer of preeminent skill that he might execute the principal works in the interior of the Temple and fabricate the various utensils intended for the sacred services. He was a master in his art or calling, and properly dignified with a title which announced his distinguished character. The title of Father, which was given to him, denotes, says Smith, the respect and esteem in which he was held, according to the similar custom of the people of the East at the present day.

I am well pleased with the suggestion of Dr. McClintock that "Hiram my father seems to mean Hiram my counsellor; that is to say, foreman or master workman"

Applying this meaning to the passages in Chronicles which refer to this artist, we shall see how easily every difficulty is removed and the Craftsman Hiram placed in his true light.

When King Hiram, wishing to aid the King of Israel in his contemplated building, writes him a letter in which he promises to comply with the request of Solomon to send him timber from Lebanon and wood-cutters to hew it, as an additional mark of his friendship and his desire to contribute his aid in building "a house for Jehovah," he gives him the services of one of his most skillful artisans and announces the gift in these words: "And now I have sent a skillful man, endued with understanding, my master workman Hiram."

And when the historian who wrote the Chronicles of the kingdom had recapitulated all the work that Hiram had accomplished, such as the pillars of the porch, the lavers and the candlesticks, and the sacred vessels, he concludes by saying that all these things were made for King Solomon by his master-workman Hiram, in the Hebrew gnasah Huram Abif Lammelech Schelomoh.

Hiram or Huram was his proper name. Ab, father of his trade or master-workman, his title, and i or if, any or his, the possessive pronominal suffix, used according to circumstances. The King of Tyre calls him Hiram Abi, "my master-workman." When the chronicler speaks of him in his relation to King Solomon, he calls him Hiram Abif "his master-workman." And as all his Masonic relations are with Solomon, this latter designation has been adopted, from Anderson, by the Craft.

Having thus disposed of the name and title of the personage who constitutes the main point in this Masonic Legend, I proceed to an examination of the origin and progressive growth of the myth.

"The Legend of the Temple-Builder," as he is commonly but improperly called, is so intimately connected in the ritual with the symbolic history of the Temple, that we would very naturally be led to suppose that the one has always been contemporary and coexistent with the other. The evidence on this point is, however, by no means conclusive or satisfactory, though a critical examination of the old manuscripts would seem to show that the writers of those documents, while compiling from traditional sources the Legend of the Craft, were not altogether ignorant of the rank and services that have been subsequently attributed by the Speculative Masons of the present day to Hiram Abif. They certainly had some notion that in the building of the Temple at Jerusalem King Solomon had the assistance of a skillful artist who had been supplied to him by the King of Tyre.

The origin of the Legend must be looked for in the Scriptural account of the building of the Temple of Jerusalem, The story, as told in the books of Kings and Chronicles, is to this effect. On the death of King David, his son and successor, Solomon, resolved to carry into execution his father's long-contemplated design of erecting a Temple on Mount Moriah for the worship of Jehovah. But the Jews were not a nation of artisans, but rather of agriculturists, and had, even in the time of David, depended on the aid of the Phoenicians in the construction of the house built for that monarch at the beginning of his reign. Solomon, therefore, applied to his ally, Hiram, King of Tyre, to furnish him with trees from Lebanon and with hewers to prepare them, for, as he said in his letter to the Tyrian King, "thou knowest that there is not any among us that can skill to hew timber like unto the Sidonians." Hiram complied with his request, and exchanged the skilled workmen of sterile Phoenicia for the oil and corn and wine of more fertile Judea.

Among the artists who were sent by the King of Tyre to the King of Israel, was one whose appearance at Jerusalem seems to have been in response to the following application of Solomon, recorded in the second book of Chronicles, the second chapter, seventh verse: "Send me now therefore a man cunning to work in gold, and in silver, and in brass, and in iron, and in purple and in crimson, and blue, and that can skill to grave with the cunning men that are with me in Judah, and in Jerusalem, whom David my father did provide."

In the epistle of King Hiram, responsive to this request,

contained in the same book and chapter, in the thirteenth and fourteenth verses, are the following words:

"And now I have sent a cunning man, endued with understanding, of Huram my father's. The son of a woman of the daughters of Dan, and his father was a man of Tyre, skillful to work in gold and in silver, in brass, in iron, in stone, and in timber, in purple, in blue, and in fine linen, and in crimson; also to grave any manner of graving, and to find out every device which shall be put to him, with thy cunning men, and with the cunning men of my lord David, thy father."

A further description of him is given in the seventh chapter of the first book of Kings, in the thirteenth and fourteenth verses, and in these words

"And King Solomon sent and fetched Hiram out of Tyre. He was a widow's son of the tribe of Naphtali-and his father was a man of Tyre, a worker in brass; and he was filled with wisdom and understanding, and cunning to work all works in brass, and he came to King Solomon and wrought all his work."

It is very evident that this was the origin of the Legend which was incorporated into the Masonic system, and which, on the institution of Speculative Freemasonry, was adopted as the most prominent portion of the Third Degree.

The mediaeval Masons were acquainted with the fact that King Solomon had an assistant in the works of the Temple, and that assistant had been sent to him by King Hiram. But there was considerable confusion in their minds upon the subject, and an ignorance of the scriptural name and attributes of the person. In the Halliwell MS., the earliest known to us, the Legend is not related. Either the writers of the two poems of which that manuscript is composed were ignorant of it, or in the combination of the two poems there has been a mutilation and the Hiramic Legend has been omitted.

In the Cooke MS., which is a hundred years later, we meet with the first allusion to it and the first error, which is repeated in various forms in all the subsequent manuscript constitutions. That manuscript says: "And at the makyng of the temple in Salamonis tyme as lit is seyd in the bibull in the iii boke of Regum in tertio Regum capitulo quinto, that Salomoii had iiii score thousand masons at his werke. And the kyngis sone of Tyry was his master mason."

The reference here made to the third book of Kings is according to the old distribution of the Hebrew canon, where the two books of Samuel are caged the mat and second books of Kings. According to our present canon, the reference would be to the fifth chapter of the first book of Kings. In that chapter nothing is said of Hiram Abif, but it is recorded there that "Adoniram was over the levy."

Now the literal meaning of Adoniram is the lord Hiram. As the King of Tyre had promised to send his workmen to Lebanon, and as it is stated that Adoniram superintended the men who were there hewing the trees, the old legendist, not taking into account that the levy of thirty thousand, over whom Adoniram presided, were Israelites and not Phoenicians, but supposing that they had been sent to Lebanon by Hiram, King of Tyre, and that he had sent Adoniram with them and viewing the word as meaning the lord Hiram, hastily came to the conclusion that this Lord or Prince Hiram was the son of the King. And hence he made the mistake of saying that the son of the King of Tyre was the person sent to Solomon to be his, master-mason or master-builder.

This error was repeated in nearly all the succeeding manuscripts, for they are really only copies of each other, and the word Adon, as meaning lord or prince, seems to have been always assumed in some one or other corrupted form as the name of the workman sent by King Hiram to King Solomon, and whom the Freemasons of the present day know as Hiram Abif.

Thus in the Doweled MS., conjecturally dated at A.D. 1550, it is said:

"And furthermore there was a Kinge of another region that men called IRAM, and he loved well Kinge Solomon and he gave him tymber to his worke. And he had a sonn that height (was called) AYNON, and he was a Master of Geometrie and was chief Master of all his Masons, and was Master of all his gravings and carvings and of all manner of Masonrye that longed to the Temple."

There can be no doubt that Aynon is here a corruption of Adon. In the Landsdowne MS., whose date is A.D. 1560, the language is precisely the same, except that it says King Iram "had a sonne that was called a man."

It seems almost certain that the initial letter a in this name has been, by careless writing, dislocated from the remaining letters, man, and that the true reading is Aman, which is itself an error, instead of Amon, and this a manifest corruption of Adon. This is confirmed by the York MS., Number 1 which is about forty years later (A.D.1600), where the name is spelled Amon. This is also the name in the Lodge of Hope MS., dated A.D. 1680.

In the Grand Lodge MS., date of A.D. 1632, he is again called the son of the King of Tyre, but his name is given as Aynone, another corrupted form of Adon. In the Sloane MS., Number 3,848, A.D. 1646, it is Aynon, the final e being omitted. In the Harleian MS., Number 1942, dated A.D. 1670, both the final e and the medial y are omitted, and the name becoming Anon approximates still nearer to the true Adon.

In the Alnwick MS., of A.D. 1701, the name is still further corrupted into Ajuon. In all of these manuscripts the Legend continues to call this artist the son of the King of Tyre, whose name is said to be Hiram or more usually Iram; and hence the corrupted orthography of Amon, Aynon, or Anon, being restored to the true form of Adon, with which word the old Masons were acquainted, as signifying Lord or Prince, we get, by prefixing it to his father's name, Adon-Iram or Adoniram, the Lord or Prince Hiram. And hence arose the mistake of confounding Hiram Abif with Adoniram, the chief of the workmen on Mount Lebanon, who was a very different person.

The Papworth MS., whose date is A. D. 1714, is too near

the time of the Revival and the real establishment of Speculative Masonry to be of much value in this inquiry. It, however, retains the statement from the Old Legend, that the artist was the son of King Hiram. But it changes his name to that of Benaim. This is probably an incorrect inflection of the Hebrew word Boneh, a builder, and shows that the writer, in an attempt to correct the error of the preceding legendists who had corrupted Adon into Anon or Amon, or Ajuon, had in his smattering of Hebrew committed a greater one.

The Krause MS. is utterly worthless as authority. It is a forgery, written most probably, I think I may say certainly, after the publication of the first edition of Anderson's Constitutions, and, of course, takes the name from that work.

The name of Hiram Abif is first introduced to public notice by Anderson in 1723 in the book of Constitutions printed in that year. In this work he changes the statement made in the Legend of the Craft, and says that the King of Tyre sent to King Solomon his namesake Hiram Abif, the prince of architects.

Then quoting in the original Hebrew a passage from the second book of Chronicles, where the name of Hiram Abif is to be found, he excels it "by allowing the word Abif to be the surname of Hiram the Mason;" furthermore he adds that in the passage where the King of Tyre calls him "Huram of my father's," the meaning is that Huram was "the chief Master Mason of my father, King Abibalus," a most uncritical attempt, because he intermixes, as its foundation, the Hebrew original and the English version. He had not discovered the true explication, namely, that Hiram is the name, and Ab the title, denoting, as I have before said, Master Workman, and that in, or iv, or if, is a pronominal suffix, meaning his, so that when speaking of him in his relation to King Solomon, he is called Hiram Abif, that is Hiram, his or Solomon's Master Workman.

But Anderson introduced an entirely new element in the Legend when he said, in the same book, that "the wise King Solomon was Grand Master of the Lodge at Jerusalem, King Hiram was Grand Master of the Lodge at Tyre, and the inspired Hiram Abif was Master of Work." In the second or 1738 edition of the Constitutions, Anderson considerably enlarged the Legend, for reasons that will be adverted to when I come, in the next part of this work, to treat of the origin of the Third Degree, but on which it is here unnecessary to dwell.

In that second edition, he asserts that the tradition is that King Hiram had been Grand Master of all Masons, but that when the Temple was finished he surrendered the pre-eminence to King Solomon. No such tradition, nor any allusion to it, is to be found in any of the Old Records now extant, and it is, moreover, entirely opposed by the current of opinion of all subsequent Masonic writers. From these suggestions of Anderson, and from some others of a more esoteric character, made, it is supposed, by him and by Dr. Desaguliers about the time of the Revival, we derive that form of the Legend of Hiram Abif which has been preserved to the present day with singular uniformity by the Freemasons of all countries.

The substance of the Legend, so far as it is concerned in

the present investigation, is that at the building of the Temple there were three Grand Masters-Solomon, King of Israel; Hiram, King of Tyre, and Hiram Abif, and that the last was the architect or chief builder of the edifice.

As what relates to the fate of Hiram Abif is to be explained in an altogether allegorical or symbolical sense, it will more appropriately come finder consideration when we are treating, in a subsequent part of this work, of the Symbolism of Freemasonry. Our present study will be the legendary character of Hiram Abif as the chief Master Mason of the Temple, and our investigations will be directed to the origin and meaning of the myth which has now, by universal consent of the Craft, been adopted, whether correctly or not we shall see hereafter.

The question before us, let it be understood, is not as to the historic truth of the Hiramic legend, as set forth in the Third Degree of the Masonic ritual-not as to whether this be the narrative of an actual occurrence or merely an allegory accompanied by a moral signification-not as to the truth or fallacy of the theory which finds the origin of Freemasonry in the Temple of Jerusalem-but how it has been that the Masons of the Middle Ages should have incorporated into their Legend of the Craft the idea that a worker in metal-in plain words, a smith-was the chief builder at the Temple. This thought, and this thought alone, must govern us in the whole course of our inquiry.

Of all the myths that have prevailed among the peoples of the earth, hardly any has had a greater antiquity or a more extensive existence than that of the Smith who worked in metals, and fabricated shields and swords for warriors, or jewelry for queens and noble ladies. Such a myth is to be found among the traditions of the earliest religions, and being handed down through ages of popular transmission, it is preserved, with various natural modifications, in the legends of the Middle Age, from Scandinavia to the most southern limit of the Latin race. Long before this period it was to be found in the mythology and the folk-lore of Assyria, of India, of Greece, and of Rome.

Freemasonry, in its most recent form as well as in its older Legend, while adopting the story of Hiram Abif, once called Adon Hiram, has strangely distorted its true features, as exhibited in the books of Kings and Chronicles; and it has, without any historical authority, transformed the Scriptural idea of a skillful smith into that of an architect and builder. Hence, in the Old Legend he is styled a "Master of Geometry and of all Masonry," and in the modern ritual of Speculative Masonry he is called "the Builder," and to him, in both, is supposed to have been entrusted the superintendence of the Temple of Solomon, during its construction, and the government and control of those workmen -the stone squarers and masons- who were engaged in the labor of its erection.

To divest this Legend of its corrupt form, and to give to Hiram Abif, who was actually an historic personage, his true position among the workmen at the Temple, can not affect, in the slightest degree, the symbolism of which he forms so integral a part, while it will rationally account for the importance that has been attributed to him in the old as well as in the new Masonic system.

Whether we make Hiram Abif the chief Builder and the Operative Grand Master of Solomon's Temple, or whether we assign that position to Anon, Amon, or Ajuon, as it is in the Old Legend, or to Adoniram, as it is done in some Masonic Rites, the symbolism will remain unaffected, because the symbolic idea rests on the fact of a Chief Builder having existed, and it is immaterial to the development of the symbolism what was his true name. The instruction intended to be conveyed in the legend of the Third Degree must remain unchanged, no matter whom we may identify as its hero; for he truly represents neither Hiram nor Anon nor Adoniram nor any other individual person, but rather the idea of man in an abstract sense,

It is, however, important to the truth of history that the real facts should be eliminated out of the mythical statements which envelop them. We must throw off the husk, that we may get at the germ. And besides, it will add a new attraction to the system of Masonic ritualism if we shall be able to trace in it any remnant of that oldest and most interesting of the myths, the Legend of the Smith, which, as I have said, has universally prevailed in the most ancient forms of religious faith.

Before investigating this Legend of the Smith in its reference to Freemasonry and to this particular Legend of Hiram Abif which we are now considering, it will be proper to inquire into the character of the Legend as it existed in the old religions and in the mediaeval myths. We may then inquire how this Legend, adopted in Freemasonry in its stricter ancient form of the Legend of Tubal Cain, became afterward confounded with another legend of a Temple-Builder.

If we go back to the oldest of all mythologies, that which is taught in the Vedic hymns, we shall find the fire-god Agni, whose flames are described as being luminous, powerful, fearful, and not to be trusted.

The element of fire thus worshipped by the primeval Aryans, as an instrument of good or of evil, was subsequently personified by the Greeks: the Vedic hymns, referring to the continual renovation of the flame, as it was fed by fuel, called it the fire-god Agni; also Gavishtha, that is, the ever young. From this the Greeks got their Hephaestus, the mighty workman, the immortal smith who forged the weapons of the gods, and, at the prayer of Thetis, fabricated the irresistible armor of Achilles. The Romans were indebted to their Aryan ancestors for the same idea of the potency of fire, and personified it in their Vulcan, a name which is evidently derived from the Sanskrit Ulka, a firebrand, although a similarity of sound has led many etymologists to deduce the Roman Vulcan from the Semitic Tubal Cain. Indeed, until the modern discoveries in comparative philology, this was the universal opinion of the learned.

Among the Babylonians an important god was Bil-can. He was the fire-god, and the name seems to be derived from Baal, or Bel, and Cain, the god of smiths, or the master smith.

George Smith, in his Chaldaen Account of Genesis, thinks that there is possibly some connection here with the Biblical Tubal Cain and the classical Vulcan.

From the fragments of Sanchoniathon we learn that the Phoenicians had a hero whom he calls Chrysor. He was worshipped after his death, in consequence of the many inventions that he bestowed on man, under the name of Diamichius; that is, the great inventor. To him was ascribed the invention of all those arts which the Greeks attributed to Hephaestus, and the Romans to Vulcan. Bishop Cumberland derives the name of Chrysor from the Hebrew Charatz, or the Sharbener, an appropriate designation of one who taught the use of iron tools. The authorized version of Genesis, which calls Tubal Cain "an instructor of every artificer in brass and iron," is better rendered in the Septuagint and the Vulgate as a sharpener of every instrument in brass and iron.

Tubal Cain has been derived, in the English lectures of Dr. Hemming, and, of course, by Dr. Oliver, from a generally received etymology that Cain meant worldly possessions, and the true symbolism of the name has been thus perverted. The true derivation is from kin, which, says Gesenius, has the especial meaning to forge iron, whence comes Kain, a spear or lance, an instrument of iron that has been forged. In the cognate Arabic it is Kayin.

"This word," says Dr. Goldziher in his work on Mythology Among the Hebrews, which with other synonymous names of trades occurs several times on the so-called Nabatean Sinaitic inscriptions, signifies Smith, maker of agricultural implements and has preserved this meaning in the Arabic Kayin and the Aramaic kinaya, whilst in the later Hebrew it was lost altogether, being probably suppressed through the Biblical attempt to derive the proper name Cain etymologically from kana, "to gain." Here it is that Hemming and Oliver got their false symbolism of "worldly possessions."

Goldziher attempts to identify mythologically Cain the fratricide with the son of Lamech. Whether he be correct or not in his theory, it is at least a curious coincidence that Cain, which I have shown to mean a smith, should have been the first builder of a city, and that the same name should have been assigned to the first forger of metals, while the old Masonic Legend makes the master smith, Hiram of Tyre, also the chief builder of Solomon. It will, I think, be interesting to trace the progress of the myth which has given in every age and every country this prominent position among artisans to the smith.

Hephaestus, or Vulcan, kindling his forges in the isle of Lemnos, and with his Cyclops journeymen beating out and shaping and welding the red-hot iron into the forms of spears and javelins and helmets and coats of mail, was the southern development of the Aryan firegod Agni. "Hephaestus, or Vulcan," says Diodorus Siculus, " was the first founder in iron, brass, gold, silver, and all fusible metals, and he taught the uses to which fire might be applied by artificers." Hence he was called by the ancients the god of blacksmiths.

The Scandinavians, or northern descendants of the Aryan

race, brought with them, in their emigration from Caucasus, the same reverence for fire and for the working of metals by its potent use. They did not, however, bring with them such recollections of Agni as would invent a god of fire

Eke the Hephaestus and Vulcan of the Greeks and Romans. They had, indeed, Loki, who derived his name, it is said by some, from the Icelandic logi, or flame.

He confines the expression to "agricultural" to enforce a particular theory then under consideration. He might correctly have been more general and included all other kinds of implements, warlike and mechanical as well as agricultural.

But he was an evil principle, and represented rather the destructive than the creative powers of fire.

But the Scandinavians, interpolating, like all the northern nations, their folk-lore into their mythology, invented their legends of a skillful smith, beneath whose mighty blows upon the yielding iron swords of marvelous keenness and strength were forged, or by whose wonderful artistic skill diadems and bracelets and jewels of surpassing beauty were constructed. Hence the myth of a wonderfully cunning artist was found everywhere, and the Legend of the Smith became the common property of all the Scandinavian and Teutonic nations, and was of so impressive a character that it continued to exist down to mediaeval times, and traces of it have extended to the superstitions of the present day. May we not justly look to its influence for the prominence given by the old Masonic legendists to the Master Smith of King Hiram among the workmen of Solomon?

Among the Scandinavians we have the Legend of Volund, whose story is recited in the Volunddarkvitha, or Lay of Volund, contained in the Edda of Saemund. Volund (pronounced as if spelled Wayland) was one of three brothers, sons of an Elf-king ; that is to say, of a supernatural race. The three brothers emigrated to Ulfdal, where they married three Valkyries, or choosers of the slain, maidens of celestial origin, the attendants of Odin, and whose attributes were similar to those of the Greek Parcae, or Fates. After seven years the three wives fled away to pursue their allotted duty of visiting battle-fields. Two of the brothers went in search of their errant wives; but Volund remained in Ulfdal. He was a skillful workman at the forge, and occupied his time in fabricating works in gold and steel, while patiently awaiting the promised return of his beloved spouse.

Niduth, the king of the country, having heard of the wonderful skill of Volund as a forger of metals, visited his home during his absence and surreptitiously got possession of some of the jewels which he had made, and of the beautiful sword which the smith had fabricated for himself

Volund, on his return, was seized by the warriors of Niduth and conducted to the castle. There the queen, terrified at his fierce looks, ordered him to be hamstrung. Thus, maimed and deprived of the power of escape or resistance, he was confined to a small island in the vicinity of the royal residence and compelled to fabricate jewels for the queen and her daughter, and weapons of war for the king.

It were tedious to recount all the adventures of the smith while confined in his island prison. It is sufficient to say that, having constructed a pair of wings by which he was enabled to fly (by which we are reminded of the Greek fable of Daedalus), he made his escape, having by stratagem first dishonored the princess and slain her two brothers.

This legend of "a curious and cunning workman" at the forge was so popular in Scandinavia that it extended into other countries, where the Legend of the Smith presents itself under various, modifications

In the Icelandic legend Volund is described as a great artist in the fabrication of iron, gold and silver. It does not, however, connect him with supernatural beings, but attributes to him great skill in his art, in which he is assisted by the power of magic. The Germans had the same legend at a very early period. In the German Legend the artificer is called Wieland, and he is represented as the son of a giant named Wade. He acquires the art of a smith from Minner, a skillful workman, and is perfected by the Dwarfs in all his operations at the forge as an armorer and goldsmith.

He goes of his own accord to the king, who is here called Nidung, where he finds another skillful smith, named Amilias, with whom he contends in battle, and kills him with his sword, Mimung. For this offense he is maimed by the king, and then the rest of the story proceeds very much like that of the Scandinavian legend. Among the Anglo-Saxons the legend is found not varying much from the original type. The story where the hero receives the name of Weland is contained in an ancient poem, of which fragments, unfortunately, only remain. The legend had become so familiar to the people that in the metrical romance of Beowulf the coat of mail of the hero is described as the work of Weland; and King Alfred in his translation of the Consolation of Philosophy by Boethius, where the author allude to the bones of the Consul Fabricius, in the passage "ubi sunt ossa Fabricie?" (where now are the bones of Fabricius?), thus paraphrases the question: Where now are the bones of the wise Weland, the goldsmith that was formerly so famed? Geoffrey of Monmouth afterward, in a Latin poem, speaks of the gold, and jewels, and cups that had been sculptured by Weland, which name he Latinizes as Gueilandus.

In the old French chronicles we repeatedly encounter the legend of the skillful smith, though, as might be expected, the name undergoes many changes. Thus, in a poem of the 6th century, entitled Gautier a la main forte, or Walter of the strong hand, it is said that in a combat of Walter de Varkastein he was protected from the lance of Randolf by a cuirass made by Wieland.

Another chronicle, of the 12th century, tells us that a Count of Angouleme, in a battle with the Normans, cut the cuirass and the body of the Norman King in twain at a single stroke, with his sword Durissima, which had been made by the smith Walander. A chronicle of the same period, written by the monk John of Marmontier, describes the magnificent habiliments of

Geoffrey Plantagenet, Duke of Normandy, among which, says the author, was "a sword taken from the royal treasury and long since renowned. Galannus, the most skillful of armorers, had employed much labor and care in making it." Galans, for Walans (the G being substituted for the W, as a letter unknown in the French alphabet), is the name bestowed in general on this skillful smith, and the romances of the Trouveres and Troubadours of northern and southern France, in the 12th and 13th centuries, abound in references to swords of wondrous keenness and strength that were forged by him for the knights and paladins.

Whether the name was given as Volund, or Wieland, or Weland, or Galans, it found its common origin in the Icelandic Volund, which signifies a smith. It is a generic term, from which the mythical name has been derived. So the Greeks called the skillful workman, the smith of their folk-lore, Daedalus, because there is a verb in their language daidallo, which means to do skillful or ornamental work.

Here it may not be irrelevant to notice the curious fact that concurrently with these legends of a skillful smith there ran in the Middle Ages others, of which King Solomon was the subject. In many of these old romances and metrical tales, a skill was attributed to him which makes him the rival of the subordinate artisan. Indeed, the artistic reputation of Solomon was so proverbial at the very time when these legends of the smith were prevalent, that in the poems of those days we meet with repeated uses of the expression "l'uevre Salemon," or "the work of Solomon," to indicate any production of great artistic beauty.

So fully had the Scandinavian sagas the German chronicles, and the French romances spoken of this mythical smith that the idea became familiar to the common people, and was handed down in the popular superstitions and the folk-lore, to a comparatively modern period. Two of these, one from Germany and one from England, will suffice as examples, and show the general identity of the legends and the probability of their common origin.

Herman Harrys, in his Tales and Legends of Lower Saxony, tells the story of a smith who dwelt in the village of Hagen, on the side of a mountain, about two miles from Osnabruck. He was celebrated for his skill in forging metals; but, being discontented with his lot, and murmuring against God, he was supernaturally carried into a cavernous cleft of the mountain, where he was condemned to be a metal king, and, resting by day, to labor at night at the forge for the benefit of men, until the mine in the mountain should cease to be productive.

In the coolness of the mine, says the legend, his good disposition returned, and he labored with great assiduity, extracting ore from its veins, and at first forging household and agricultural implements. Afterward he confined himself to the shoeing of horses for the neighboring; farmers. In front of the cavern was a stake fixed in the ground, to which the countryman fastened the horse which he wished to have shod, and on a stone nearby he laid the necessary fee. He then retired. On returning in due time he would find the task completed; but the smith, or, as he was called, the Hiller, i.e., Hider, would never permit himself to be seen.

Similar to this is the English legend, which tells us that in a vale of Berkshire, at the foot of White Horse Hill, evidently, from the stones which lay scattered around, the site of a Druidic monument, formerly dwelt a person named Wayland Smith. It is easily understood that here the handicraft title has been incorporated with the anglicized name, and that it is the same as the mediaeval Weland the Smith. No one ever saw him, for the huge stones afforded him a hiding-place. He, too, was a Hiller,- for the word in the preceding legend does not mean "the man of the hill," but is from the German hullen, to cover or conceal, and denotes the man who conceals himself. In this studious concealment of their persons by both of these smiths we detect the common origin of the two legends. When his services were required to shoe a horse, the animal was left among the stones and a piece of money placed on one of them. The owner then retired, and after some time had elapsed he returned, when he found that the horse was shod and the money had disappeared. The English reader ought to be familiar with this story from the use made of it by Sir Walter Scott in his novel of Kenilworth.

It is very evident, from all that has been here said, that the smith, as the fabricator of weapons for the battle-field and jewels for the bourdoir, as well as implements of agriculture and household use, was a most important personage in the earliest times, deified by the ancients, and invested by the moderns with supernatural gifts. It is equally evident that this respect for the smith as an artificer was prevalent in the Middle Ages. But in the very latest legends, by a customary process of degeneration in all traditions, when the stream becomes muddled as it proceeds onward, he descended in character from a forger of swords, his earliest occupation, to be a shoer of horses, which was his last. It must be borne in mind also, that in the -Middle Ages the respect for the smith as a "curious and cunning" workman began by the introduction of a new clement, brought by the Crusaders and pilgrims from the East to be shared with King Solomon, who was supposed to be invested with equal skill.

It is not, therefore, strange that the idea should have been incorporated into the rituals of the various secret societies of the Middle Ages and adopted by the Freemasonry at first by the Operative branch and afterward, in a more enlarged form, by the Speculative Masons.

In all of the old manuscripts constitutions of the Operative Masons we find the Legendof the Craft, and with it, except in one instance, and that the earliest, a reference to Tubal Cain as the one who "found [that is, invented] the Smith Craft of gold and silver, iron and copper and steel."

Nothing but the universal prevalence of the mediaeval legend of the smith, Volund or Weland, can, I think, account for this reference to the Father of Smith Craft in a legend which should have been exclusively appropriated to Stone Craft. There is no connection between the forge and the trowel which authorized on any other ground the honor paid by stonemasons to a forger of metals-an honor so marked that in time the very name of Tubal Cain came to be adopted as a significant and important word in the Masonic ritual, and the highest place in the traditional labors of the Temple was assigned to a worker in gold and brass and iron.

Afterward, when the Operative Art was superseded by the Speculative Science, the latter supplemented to the simple Legend of the Craft the more recondite Legend of the Temple. In this latter Legend, the name of that Hiram whom the King of Tyre had sent with all honor to the King of Israel, to give him aid in the construction of the Temple, is first introduced under his biblical appellation. But this is not the first time that this personage is made known to the fraternity. In the older Legends he is mentioned, always with a different name but always, also as "King Solomon's Master Mason."

In the beginning of the 18th century, when what has been called the Revival took place, there was a continuation of the general idea that he was the chief Mason at the Temple; but the true name of Hiram Abif is, as we have already said, then first found in a written or printed record. Anderson speaks of his architectural abilities in exaggerated terms. He calls him in one place "the most accomplished Mason on earth," and in another "the prince of architects." This character has adhered to him in all subsequent times, and the unwritten Legend of the present day represents him as the, Chief Builder of the Temple, the "Operative Grand Master," and the "Skillful Architect" by whose elaborate designs on his trestle-board the Craft were guided in their labors and the edifice was constructed.

Now, it will be profitable in the investigation of historic truth to compare these attributes assigned to Hiram Abif by the older and more recent legendists with the biblical accounts of the same person which have already been cited.

In the original Hebrew text of the passage in the book of Chronicles, the words which designate the profession of Hiram Abif are Khoresh nekhoshet,- literally, a worker in brass. The Vulgate, which was the popular version in those days and from which the old legendists must have derived their knowledge of biblical history, thus translates the letter of King Hiram to King Solomon:

"Therefore I have sent to thee a wise and most skillful man, Hiram the workman or smith, my father -Hiram fabrem Patrem meum. Indeed, in the close of the verse in the Authorized Version he is described as being "cunning to work all works in brass." And hence Dr. Adam Clarke, in his Commentaries, calls him "a very intelligent coppersmith."

The error into which the old legendists and the modern Masonic writers have fallen, in supposing him to have been a stone-mason or an architect, has arisen from the mistranslation in the Authorized Version of the passage in Chronicles where he is said to have been "skillful to work in gold and in silver, in brass, in iron, in stone, and in timber." The words in the original are Baabanim vebagnelsim, in stones and in woods,- that is, in precious stones and in woods of various kinds. That is to say, besides being a coppersmith he was a lapidary and a carver and gilder. The words in the original Hebrew are in the plural, and

73

therefore the translation "in wood and in timber" is not correct. Gesenius says-and there is no better authority for a Hebraism- that the word eben is used by way of excellence, to denote a precious stone, and its plural, abanim, means, therefore, precious stones. In the same way gnetz, which in the singular signifies a tree, in the plural denotes materials of wood, for any purpose.

The work that was done by Hiram Abif in the Temple is fully recounted in the first book of Kings, the seventh chapter, from the fifteenth to the fortieth verse, and is briefly recapitulated in verses forty-one to fifty. It is also enumerated in the third and fourth chapters of second Chronicles, and in both books care is taken to say that when this work was done the task of Hiram Abif was completed. In the first book of Kings (vii. 40) it is said:

"So Hiram made an end of dung all the work that he made King Solomon for the house of the Lord." In the second book of Chronicles (iv. 2) the statement is repeated thus: "And Hiram finished the work that he was to make for King Solomon for the house of God."

The same authority leaves us in no doubt as to what that work was to which the skill of Hiram Abif had been devoted. "It was," says the book of Chronicles, "the two pillars, and the pommels and the chapiters which were on the top of the pillars; and four hundred pomegranates on the two wreaths; two rows of pomegranates on each wreath, to cover the two pommels of the chapiters which were upon the pillars. He made also bases, and lavers made he upon the bases; one sea and twelve oxen under it. The pots also, and the shovels and the flesh hooks and all their instruments, did Huram his father (Hiram Abif) make to King Solomon, for the house of the Lord, of bright brass."

Enough has been said to show that the labors of Hiram Abif in the Temple were those of a worker in brass and in precious stones, in carving and in gilding, and not those of a stonemason. He was the decorator and not the builder of the Temple. He owes the position which he holds in the legends and in the ritual of Freemasonry, not to any connection which he had with the art of architecture, of which there is not the slightest mention by the biblical authorities, but like Tubal Cain, to his skill in bringing the potency of fire under his control and applying it to the forging of metals.

The high honor paid to him is the result of the influence of that Legend of the Smith, so universally spread in the Middle Ages, which recounted the wondrous deeds of Volund, or Wieland, or Wayland. The smith was, in the mediaeval traditions, in the sagas of the north and in the romances of the south of Europe, the maker of swords and coats of mail; in the Legends of Freemasonry he was transmuted into the fabricator of holy vessels and sacred implements.

But the idea that of all handicrafts smith-craft was the greatest was unwittingly retained by the Masons when they elevated the skillful smith of Tyre, the "cunning" worker in brass, to the highest place as a builder in their Temple legend. The spirit of critical iconoclasm, which strips the exterior husk from the historic germ of all myths and legends, has been doing much to divest the history of Freemasonry of all fabulous assumptions. This attempt to give to Hiram Abif his true position, and to define his real profession, is in the spirit of that iconoclasm.

But the doctrine here advanced is not intended to affect in the slightest degree the part assigned to Hiram Abif in the symbolism of the Third Degree. Whatever may have been his profession, he must have stood high in the confidence of the two kings, of him who sent him and him who received him, as "a master workman;" and he might well be supposed to be entitled in an allegory to the exalted rank bestowed upon him in the Legend of the Craft and in the modern ritual.

Allegories are permitted to diverge at will from the facts of history and the teachings of science. Trees may be made to speak, as they do in the most ancient fable extant, and it is no infringement of their character that a worker in brass may be transmuted into a builder in stone to suit a symbolic purpose. Hence this "celebrated artist," as he is fairly called, whether smith or mason, is still the representative, in the symbolism of Freemasonry, of the abstract idea of man laboring in the temple of life, and the symbolic lesson of his tried integrity and his unhappy fate is still the same.

As Freemasons, when we view the whole Legend as a myth intended to give expression to a symbolic idea, we may be content to call him an architect, the first of Masons, and the chief builder of the Temple; but as students of history we can know nothing of him and admit nothing concerning him that is not supported by authentic and undisputed authority.

We must, therefore, look upon him as the ingenious artist, who worked in metals and in precious stones, who carved in cedar and in olive-wood, and thus made the ornaments of the Temple.

He is only the Volund or Wieland of the olden legend, changed, by a mistaken but a natural process of transmuting traditions, from a worker in brass to a worker in stone.